Managing Stress and Anxiety

By

Alexander R. Tipton MA.

Licensed Professional Counselor

Also by Alexander R. Tipton:

The Fifth Age: Book One – The Tournament

The Fifth Age: Book Two – Fire and Ice

The Fifth Age: Book Three – Fall of the Paladin

The Fifth Age: Book Four – The Heavens Will Quake

Loveless: Book One

For More information on the Author, the Series, or upcoming Titles, visit the Author's website at www.Tiptonbooks.webs.com or on Facebook at Facebook.com/AlexanderRTipton

Anxiety has met its match.
In the following pages you will follow along with Alexander R. Tipton, a Licensed Professional Counselor and Therapist, who will guide you through multiple strategies for improving, managing, and taking control of your anxiety.
The book first covers a basic understanding of what anxiety is, where it comes from and how it impacts the human body.
From there you will get your hands dirty, so to speak, by utilizing supplied materials to immediately put strategies into action with a 30 day series of specific homework assignments designed specifically to improve anxiety and stress management. These activities will create a level of control for anxiety management.

The book offers researched and time-tested strategies for reducing and controlling anxiety and stress. That said, it should not take the place of medical or other in-person mental health advice. This book exists solely for the purpose of self help and any advice or action taken as a result of this book is purely at the will/discretion of the reader. By taking part, the reader releases the author and distributor of all legal or ethical liability for any harm or damages that may result as a consequence of the information and homework assigned.

Are you ready to make a positive and fulfilling difference in your life by taking control of stress and anxiety?

Read on for the journey.

Table of Contents

Introduction..6

Johari's Window (Activity)........................10

Stopping an Anxiety Attack.........................14

Breathing..16

Body Tension and Reduction (Activity)..........18

Distraction...20

Visualization..21

Eliminating Anxiety Through Planning (Activity).22

Medication..27

Additional Ideas to Consider.......................28

Daily Homework (Activity)..........................30

References...81

Anxiety is a Menace

The human body has many self-defense mechanisms built into its various systems. When confronted by a fear inducing stimulus, the body reacts by going into what is called the fight or flight reaction. When this happens, the heart rate increases, adrenaline is pumped into the bloodstream, and most non-vital systems are switched off in an attempt to fully prepare the body to fight off the stimulus or retreat as quickly as possible from it. One could see such a defense mechanism as being very important for a cave man who is confronted by a saber-toothed tiger. However, in today's world a person is much less likely to run into a life or death stimulus.

When worry, stress, and anxiety all come together the body may have a similar reaction, yet there is no aversive stimulus that can be fought or retreated from. When such a bodily reaction happens to a non-dangerous stimulus it is called a panic attack.

According to the American Psychiatric Association (2013) a panic attack is a short period in which there is a feeling of complete fear, dread, or doom. Such attacks are accompanied by symptoms that include but are not limited to: shortness of breath, heart palpitations, chest pain or discomfort, stomach nausea, dry heaving or vomiting, choking, or fear of going crazy or losing control.

In our modern world we face many challenges that our ancestors never dreamed of. Through evolution and advancement, our species have eliminated many obstacles. Now in order to survive, we face a totally different world of challenges. Managing stress and anxiety is no easy feat. Anxiety, the number-one most reported mental health symptom, is a product of our modern area, and one that is here to stay.

Anxiety is fear.

Fear is one of five primary emotions that exists to serve a purpose. Fear's purpose in nature is to protect us from what could kill, or seriously harm us.

Modern psychologists refer to this "Fight or Flight" reaction by many changing and expanding names.

At any rate, the reaction to fear creates not only a mental response, but a physical one. When in a state of fear, the human body reacts, sending chemicals through the blood stream. This calls the body to action and gives it strength to handle whatever threat or fear has triggered it.

This reaction, while very beneficial to our ancestors' survival, creates many common problems in modern humans. Modern lifestyle and technology have made basic survival a distant thought. Instead, current (much more minor stressors in comparison), have become triggers for such a reaction.

Our ancestors experienced such stress reactions in order to fend off attackers, wild animals or to gain the strength to flee and escape. Its purpose: survival. The threat often ended quickly through escape, overpowering the threat, or death.

Modern stressors, however, are different. They tend to linger in the form of worry, instead of an immediate threat. When such worries are on our mind day after day, we can experience a similar effect to the fight or flight response when it feels unnecessary. This is the route that anxiety's physical symptoms begin to impact the human body.

Anxiety and panic are quite simply the body's misunderstanding in reaction to our worries.

The question is, how can we control and stop such a reaction? How can we manage our stress and anxiety in the modern world?

In the following paged we will explore several aspects of anxiety and stress reduction and then the book with finish with a 30 day series of assignments designed to practice and utilize the skills taught in this book, in your own life.

Johari's Window

Create a figure on the next page, fill in each window with the corresponding worries or thoughts that generate anxiety. Something does not have be a negative or stressor to be an anxiety. Once each window if filled, consider the placement of each.

Are there a majority of worries that cannot be controlled, are there many that are not cared about? Productive worries are those that one can control/influence as well as those in which the individual desires to make a change to or influence.

Create a chart to organize your worries and consider the results:

Draw out a grid of four window panes:

On the left, label the rows: Care about, Do not Care about, respectively. On the top, label the Columns: Control, Do Not control. You can Google Johari's window if you need help.

Add your stressors accordingly and follow the instructions:

Activity:

Using the completed chart consider what window's your anxiety/worries are most prevalent.

Do you worry about a lot of things you can't control? Do you find that many of your worries are things that don't matter much to your life yet still cause you worry?

The most productive of the 4 windows in the top left. Worries that are both controllable and cared about are those worries where one should focus most of their attention and create goals, actions steps, or eliminations.

If a worry can't be controlled than it is a part of life there must be radically accepted, somehow moved into a window of control, or eliminated in favor of other, more productive efforts.

When worries are organized into the window of caring and controlling one can begin to create action steps around improving, addressing, or influencing those worries.

Save the completed Johari's window for later in the book as there will be an activity on creating such action steps.

Stopping an Anxiety Attack

The best way to fight anxiety is to NOT fight. Anxiety is the drive to act, rush, and energetically act. The simplest way to eliminate physical feelings of anxiety is to become physically relaxed. One cannot be both physically anxious and physically relaxed at the same time.

Physical characteristics of anxiety (and panic) are often characterized by the body's call to action. This includes increased and shallow breathing, racing heartbeat, increased chemical reactions/endorphins, and an increase in energy and jitteriness. To transform an anxious body into a relaxed one, one must change their own body chemistry.

To do this, think of what causes feelings of relaxation.

Next follow the flow chart of anxiety reduction:

Stop

Sit or Lie Down

Focus on Breathing

Body Tension and

Reduction

Visualization

Distraction

Sit or lie down and close your eyes. Focus on breathing, making sure to breathe in and out slowly, thus slowing your heart rate.

Stop, sit or lie down, focus on breathing, body tension and reduction, visualization, distraction.

A Trick for Breathing

When engrossed in vigorous exercise or experiencing panic attack, your breathing is often characterized by quick and shallow inhales, followed by even faster exhales. For example: someone breathing as described may inhale for 2 seconds and exhale for 1 to 1.5 seconds.

Anxiety is the opposite of relaxed. Someone that is relaxed or sleeping breathes in much the opposite fashion; by breathing in deeply for 4 to 5 seconds and exhaling for 6-7 seconds.

When feeling panic or severe anxiety, it can help to sit or lie down and focus on breathing. In doing so, count 6 seconds inhaling and 8 seconds exhaling. By exhaling longer, your body is assured that no such rush or need to act exists. As a result, your body calms.

Inhale   Exhale

6 Seconds   8 Seconds

Depending on lung capacity, some people are capable of even longer breath cycles. It can become a fun goal to challenge yourself to lengthen breathing cycles. Inhaling for 10 seconds and exhaling for 12 seconds could be a goal. At any rate, the process not only helps regulate the breathing cycle to one of calm, but it also distracts the mind from the current panic or worry and refocuses it upon the breathing and counting.

Body Tension and Reduction

Tension and stress is often kept within your muscles. Another strategy to help manage stress and anxiety is to distract yourself through tension reduction.

To achieve tension reduction, sit or lie comfortably. Attempt to slow your breathing, then start from the base and work your way up. Tighten the foot muscles by clenching your toes to the point of discomfort. Hold this position for a few moments and then gradually release.

As you release, you should feel the tension let up. When this happens, visualize the stress leaving your body. Move up to the calves of your legs and repeat, moving up through each body muscle group, one by one. Work all the way to the shoulders, and finally the face and eyes. Hold flexed and tense muscles, only to slowly release them.

This strategy should take 5 to 10 minutes. While offering a significant distraction from anxiety provoking thoughts, it will also help ease any tension stored in your muscles.

Visualization

Another strategy to help manage severe anxiety, stress or panic is Visualization. It is often most effective when used in conjunction with breathing or body tension reduction. Visualization is an umbrella term. It can be applied to any imagining or thinking that creates an internal cognitive state of calm.

In counseling/therapy, a clinician often helps their patient create a "safe space," or visualized setting that the patient can go to in their mind when facing panic or anxiety. While using one of the other strategies, picture a calming place or a repetitive, calming action taking place. It is common to picture anxiety leaving the body in color while breathing out or releasing muscle tension.

Visualization is best used when you focus on an image or experience that is simple, calming, repetitive, and well known. It can create a sense of calm that plays to the strengths of other strategies, allowing deeper relaxation.

Distraction

It is much harder to feel anxious if you are thinking about or doing something else. This is especially true if it commands your attention more strongly than the feelings of anxiety. A good distraction is anything that pulls attention away from anxiety, allowing calming thoughts to fill your subconscious.

The best strategy is to create a preset list of distractions if anxiety or panic sets in. Such a list is often called "coping skills" or "outlets."

Take a few minutes to make a list of outlets and coping skills that you can use.

Eliminating Anxiety Through Planning

Elimination is simply the removing of an item of worry or stress. The simplest way one does this is to cross the item off the list or remove the obligation it presents. This however, is not always easy, as some stressors or items are time delayed, have barriers to completion, or are simply not under our control.

To Eliminate or Not

Many stressors shouldn't be eliminated while others simply can't be. If a stressor is something enjoyable, for instance worry about an upcoming vacation, few would want to eliminate such a fun prospect.

Fun does not always mean stress free, and many people experience stress, anxiety and worry about things they enjoy. Other examples include "beneficial stressors" such as applying to college, asking someone on a date, or a job interview. These all have the potential to lead to great experiences, yet may still cause stress or anxiety.

Other items can't be eliminated because they are obligations. You can't avoid paying bills, at least not without consequences. If you hope to keep your job, you have to show up to work. And you might have to pick up the in-laws from the airport once in a while.

These things may all cause stress, but cannot be eliminated either because their elimination would cause an even worse consequence, or it is not feasible to not get them done. These are obligations, but even they have a role in stress planning.

When faced with any stressful scenario or worry, you should ask yourself several questions. A worry is useless if it does little more than take space in your working memory (consciousness) and cause distress.

A worry is the result of stimuli that formulates our body to react. What makes this difficult is that it wants us to react instantaneously. Since most modern-day worries are prolonged, it leaves little use for the quick jerking reaction most anxiety provoking stimuli creates. Sorting and managing the worry is the answer.

The first task is to ask yourself, "Is this worry about something I will enjoy?"

If the answer is yes, then you should not eliminate it. However, you might ask, "How do I manage it then?" The answer is simple. To get such a stressor out of your working memory, you simply must schedule it. It's as easy at that.

Many people feel that they must remember anything important. Thus, they believe they must keep worrying about them. This is one way many people have taught themselves to keep important thoughts or plans in their working memory. This is a mistake.

Keeping such thoughts in your working memory creates anxiety and stress. The best strategy is to get it out of your working memory and organize it. If the stressor is to be enjoyed, then it should be planned or scheduled.

You might consider using a planner, scheduler, calendar, or even electronic devices or scratch paper. The idea is that you should somehow record the details of the idea/stress. For example: "Have drinks with Joey." Figure out the where, the when, and write it all down. "Have drinks with Joey on Friday at 8 at Gustave's." Even if you are unsure about the details, you can still plan or schedule the idea. For example: "Have drinks with Joey, Call him Monday morning at 8 to schedule."

This strategy takes the worry out of your working memory and plans/schedules it for a time that it can be done or managed.

One of the single biggest complaints from those suffering with anxiety is that they can't sleep. This strategy is excellent for that purpose. When one tosses and turns at night, it is often because of a worry or worries.

Simply jot down the worry, plan it, or make a plan of when to plan it and go to sleep. Once the idea is jotted down, it no longer becomes a worry, but a plan of action. Taking action is what anxiety's entire purpose is. Anxiety is pushing our bodies into action, so TAKE ACTION.

Medication

In many cases, a primary care doctor is the first stop when seeking medication. However, they do not specialize in psycho-active medication and may refer patients seeking medication to a specialist; most likely a psychiatric mental health nurse practitioner or a psychiatrist.

When asking the question, "Should I consider medication for my stress/anxiety?" The most clinical approach is to consider your functioning. If you have difficulty doing a daily task like going to work, class, getting out of bed, or participating in regular social situation, then it is possible that medication may be a necessary and helpful step in recovery.

Anxiety is incredibly common. However, many do not have the functioning impacts severe enough to indicate a need for medication.

If a severe infringement on daily functioning exists, such an individual should seek additional professional support.

Additional Ideas to Consider

Some important concepts to remember...

Anxiety cannot hurt you. If you reflect on every instance you experienced anxiety, what was the end result every time?

Chances are it eventually went away on its own or through some other effort.

Anxiety is temporary.

It will eventually go away and can only exist to cause discomfort. It is that discomfort that sometimes makes people fearful of anxiety, thus triggering further reactions that can make anxiety and its symptoms feel more severe.

Managing stress and anxiety and its severity is entirely under your control. By remembering this, you empower yourself to use the tools and know-how to beat anxiety and continue to beat it.

For further strategies or to fully explore ways to reduce and manage your own anxiety and stress, check out the course at

(https://www.udemy.com/course/managing-stress-and-anxiety/learn/lecture/11758924#overview)

Daily Homework

30 Days of Anxiety Reduction

Daily Homework:

The next section of the book will take you through a series of daily homework assignments, each designed to help gain control over anxiety and stress.

Assignments should be done daily, and each should be read in the morning, or the night before if reading in the morning is not possible or difficult.

Each day will have a different goal or task to practice. If a day is missed, it is best practice to pick up where you left off. However, if multiple days are missed it is recommended to begin the series over again so that a continuous 30 days of commitment is placed toward the goal of reduced anxiety and stress.

At the end of the next 30 days, you should be able to:

Breath effectively to calm panic and improve relaxation

Manage time and eliminate wasteful outlets or obligations

Try new or previously feared activities

Relax and calm a nervous body

And

Reflect on the experience and reuse any retained skills as needed.

30 Days of Anxiety Reduction

Day One: Breathing – Do every Day

Day Two: Journal Entry I

Day Three: Body Tension reduction

Day Four: Elimination

Day Five: Goals and action planning

Day Six: Totem

Day Seven: Journal Entry II

Day Eight: Eye Contact

Day Nine: Time Management

Day Ten: Brain Break

Day Eleven: Journal Entry III

Day Twelve: Fear

Day Thirteen: Stranger Danger

Day Fourteen: Gratitude

Day Fifteen: Journal Entry IV

Day Sixteen: Vision Board

Day Seventeen: Challenging Thought Worksheet

Day Eighteen: Turning Negative into Positive

Day Nineteen: Growth Experience

Day Twenty: Journal Entry V

Day Twenty-One: Face Your Fear I

Day Twenty-Two: What about My Money

Day Twenty-Three: Forgiveness

Day Twenty-Four: Comfort over Comfort

Day Twenty-Five: Silence

Day Twenty-Six: Safe Space

Day Twenty-Seven: Say No

Day Twenty-Eight: Face Your Fear II

Day Twenty-Nine: Journal Entry VI

Day Thirty: Face Your Fear III

Day One:

Breathing

The first day's assignment is to practice breathing. The cornerstone to any relaxation, calming, or coping skills when it comes to anxiety or stress reduction is breathing.

Many of the physical discomforts and body sensation that come with intense panic or anxiety are a direct result of a flaw in breathing that comes from the body's natural fight or flight reaction.

By practicing breathing today you can set yourself up for improved anxiety management across the rest of the assignments.

This first assignment is something that should be done every single day of the process. Each other day will have its own homework assignment/goal, but this assignment should also be done each and every day to help create a lasting coping skill through breathing.

<u>Activity:</u>

To start, sit comfortably. Place your feet on the floor and pull your shoulders back into straight posture.

Use your hand to cup your abdomen just below your navel. Close your eyes and breathe.

Feel your abdomen and imagine that an airbag lies within. Imagine as you breathe, that it fills and empties with air, causing your lower abdomen to expand and contract.

Breath in slowly, counting. For beginners, aim for a 5 second inhale. During the 5 seconds try to fully fill your lower abdomen. Then hold for 2 seconds, then release, breathing out slowly and counting to 6 seconds.

5 seconds in, hold for 2, and exhale for 6.

If you feel you can breathe for a longer rotation try to do 10, 2, and 12, or even longer if you have strong lungs.

Do this for several minutes while you lower your shoulders and feel your body relax.

This type of breathing, called diaphragmatic breathing, takes air deep into your body and releases it slower than it takes it in. It creates a self-soothed feeling of calm and slows the body's reactions to fear and worry down.

One can not be both anxious and relaxed at the same time. Using this scientifically proven exercise will help utilize that aspect to help create a sense of calm and relaxation.
Do this every day of the 30 day process until each assignment is complete.

Day Two:

Today make a plan to do a journal entry.

It doesn't have to be written, but at least somehow recorded. Take a few minutes to write, type, text, film, or otherwise record a personal reflection of your worries, stresses, and anxiety.

Make a mental note of how you are feeling, and the way things have been going, for better or worse.

Make note of your expectations for the next 28 days and what you hope to accomplish in that time.

Don't forget to breathe.

Day Three:

Body tension and reduction.

To achieve tension reduction, sit or lie comfortably. Attempt to slow your breathing, then start from the base and work your way up. Tighten the foot muscles by clenching your toes to the point of discomfort. Hold this position for a few moments and then gradually release.

As you release, you should feel the tension let up. When this happens, visualize the stress leaving your body. Try to assign the stress a color, and picture that color leaving your body. Move up to the calves of your legs and repeat, moving up through each body muscle group, one by one. Work all the way to the shoulders, and finally the face and eyes. Hold flexed and tense muscles, only to slowly release them.

Don't forget to breathe.

Day Four:

Elimination

Make a list of your worries. Write them down, or otherwise electronically record them in a list format. When the list of current stressors/worries is compiled, go down the list respectively asking each of the following questions.

-Will this benefit me, pay off, or otherwise improve my life/situation?

-Can this be delegated?

-Is this an obligation?

The yes or no response to each will tell you how to handle each stressor. If it will benefit, pay off or improve, determine if it is something you want to do or if it would be better to ask for help with it. If it can be delegated move it to the delegate pile. If it can't move onward. If something worried about is neither enjoyable, able to be delegated and is not an obligation then it should be eliminated and removed from a list of worries.

Worries cease to be worries when they are delegated, scheduled or planed as an action step, or eliminated entirely. Pick a pile for each and remove them as worries.

Don't forget to breathe.

Day Five:

Goals and Action Planning

The previous day you made a list to separate worries/stressors into group to be 1) eliminated, 2) delegated, or 3) action plan/scheduled.

Today take out any items that were in group 3).

An anxiety is nothing more than a worry, or a call to action, but as you have previously learned, not all anxiety can be immediately dealt with. Action planning is where you make a plan to deal with said worries.

Take each item on your list and determine what can be addressed immediately and what required planning or cannot be handled until a particular day/scenario of events.

The items that can be addressed immediately, simply open a calendar/planner and set days and times to address the given concern. Give yourself ample time with the more challenging tasks.

For the other items consider scheduling out, during a time that the worry can be addressed or even planning a "worrying session" so that the particular stressor has it's own specified time to be addressed and thought through (even if it can't be resolved yet).

By organizing each stressor to a specific day/time or multiple days and times, the stressor ceases to be simply a worry and has become an action step where you have specifically cited a time to address it.

Make your list and fill your calendar/planner to the best of your abilities.

Try to remind yourself that these were worries and now they are action steps that you are addressing.

They each have their own timeframe to be managed and do not have to be thought of or worried about until that scheduled time.

Anything that can be handled today feel free to address.

Don't forget to breathe.

Day Six:

Totem

Pick out an object. It can really be anything that will fit in a pocket that has some weight to it.

Pick something that has a texture you can identify and a shape that makes it unique. It should be identifiable with one's eyes closed and should be kept on your person during the day.

This is your Totem.

It is an object that will remind you that you are on this 30 day journey of improving anxiety and stress.

Whenever you find yourself anxious or stressed, take out the totem, spin it in you hands and feel its texture while doing your breathing exercise.

Remind yourself that anxiety is temporary and that it can't control you.

Don't forget to breathe.

Day Seven:

Today make a plan to do a journal entry.

It doesn't have to be written, but at least somehow recorded. Take a few minutes to write, type, text, film, or otherwise record a personal reflection of your worries, stresses, and anxiety.

Make a mental note of how you are feeling, and the way things have been going, for better or worse.

Reflect on the previous Journal entry and think about the progress toward your goals.

Do not forget to breathe.

Day Eight:

Eye Contact

This assignment is rather uncomfortable. Which is, in essence, the entire idea.

It can be skipped, but with the caveat that it is at least attempted.

Throughout the day, observe and make eye contact with at least 3 people. Stare directly at them for 5-7 seconds after they have made eye contact with you. This is incredibly uncomfortable for most people, but it helps create a feeling of improved confidence and control over one's reactions to feeling awkward or nervous.

Should the person react, question your staring or otherwise follow up your staring in a way that you need a quick escape, simply say:

"I'm sorry, I mistook you for a friend."

This is a very common and forgivable interaction that happens daily and removes the feeling of discomfort from both parties involved. The challenge is to maintain the staring BEFORE using this escape line. Don't forget to breathe.

Day Nine:

Time Management.

Make a drawing of a rectangular tube or container with 24 hours as the measurement. Make multiple for weekend/weekdays off/workdays/school days and account for each type of day you may have during a given week.

Break down each of the 24 hour containers into several categories.

Sleep

Work and/or School

Survival: (Bathroom, bathing, eating, dressing, and errands).

Leisure: what is left over

With each day, determine how much time is left over for leisure. Then consider how much time during the leisure time is spent either watching television/videos or spent on social media.

Consider making changes to the level of leisure time you have by modifying it to better fit your list of goals/action steps you made earlier in this process.

Even one hour a day on any given project adds considerable progress over time.

Don't forget to breathe.

Day Ten:

Brain Break

Consider taking a break from media.

For today, put down the mobile phone, tablet, and avoid other screens (except for work). Take a day's break from social media and other internet.

Take today to reflect and gauge your reactions to the absents of the technology.

Do you find it difficult or easy? Do you find that media is an escape from anxiety, or does it indirectly cause it for you?

As you reflect on your social media and technology usage today while it is set aside, consider its role in your life, and how much time and energy you put into it.

Don't forget to breathe.

Day Eleven:

Today make a plan to do a journal entry.

It doesn't have to be written, but at least somehow recorded. Take a few minutes to write, type, text, film, or otherwise record a personal reflection of your worries, stresses, and anxiety.

Make a mental note of how you are feeling, and the way things have been going, for better or worse. Reflect on the previous Journal entries and think about the progress toward your goals.

Do not forget to breathe.

Day Twelve:

Fear

Today's focus is fear. Not just the feeling of fear, but the concept.

Consider what you are afraid of. What outcomes do you most fear?

Are they things that are likely to happen, unlikely, or defiantly going to happen, or won't ever happen?

Break some of your most common and biggest fears into each of those four categories.

Consider how much time/worry you spend on each of those fears.

If a fear is inevitable, why must it consume your daily life, as all the worry in the world will not prevent it?

At the same time, if a fear is never going to happen, then why is it to be feared?

Determine the 80-20 rule. That is, what 20 percent of your fears take up 80 percent of your worry and stress. These are the fears most worth looking at and even facing when and if you are ready.

Once you lave a list and know what you fears are and how they break down, you can organize them into a strategy to eliminate, delegate, or defeat each one.

Use the strategy discussed earlier to break down each fear into a respective decision.

Don't forget to breathe.

Day Thirteen:

Stranger Danger

Today at some point you are to talk to a complete stranger, or someone you've never spoken to (note, if you work with the public, it should be outside your job functions.)

In some way interact with and talk (about the weather, the time of day, or even something personal) with a complete stranger.

Think about your reaction to this person and how you may have felt or what drew you to feel comfortable (or uncomfortable) approaching them.

Don't forget to breathe.

Day Fourteen:

Gratitude

Multiple studies show that gratitude has an incredibly positive impact on the brain.

Take a few minutes today to think about what you are grateful for. It could be who, what, when, and where.

Make a list of 10 items that you are grateful for.

Go through the list when you are satisfied with it and concentrate on each item. Say "thank you" out loud.

Relish in the fact that you are blessed with that item on the list and appreciate it.

Hang on to the list and look at it whenever you need a reminder of all that is going your way.

Don't forget to breathe.

Day Fifteen:

Today make a plan to do a journal entry.

It doesn't have to be written, but at least somehow recorded. Take a few minutes to write, type, text, film, or otherwise record a personal reflection of your worries, stresses, and anxiety.

Make a mental note of how you are feeling, and the way things have been going, for better or worse.

Reflect on the previous Journal entries and think about the progress toward your goals.

Do not forget to breathe.

Day Sixteen:

Vision Board

Remember that anxiety is a driven emotional fear to act.

Take the stress out of the desire for action and make a list.

Use a dry erase board, a piece of cardboard, a poster, or even a post it note if that is all you have, and make a list that can be posted in your bedroom.

The list should include your greatest goals.

What do you want to accomplish, where do you want to go, what do you want to do? Anything that is important for you to have, do, or experience is your life can go on the board.

It doesn't matter how impossible or easy the items seem. If they are a dream/goal, write them on the board.

Once you are done, consider how much time and money each item costs you. Write it out in terms of a monthly income and time allotment.

If one single item or experience costs a lot of money or free time, simply determine how much money you would need to make monthly to afford it and how much time you would need to devote to doing/getting it.

Break those amounts down into a monthly basis. When you consider your dreams, it is likely that the monthly amount of time and money you need brings many of those goals closer to reality.

Consider your list and appreciate that you will accomplish that list. How does it make you feel? What are your thoughts?

Don't forget to breathe.

Day Seventeen:

Challenging Thoughts Worksheet

Consider an anxious thought you have. Go through the following questions to best sort out the meaning/purpose of your worry and work through it.

What's the situation?

What am I thinking or imagining?

How much do I believe this thought? a little medium a lot (or rate 0-100%)

How does that thought make me feel? angry sad anxious other

How strong is the feeling? a little medium a lot (or rate 0-100%)

What is the evidence that makes this thought seem true?

What is the evidence that makes this thought seem false?

For those thoughts that may have been formed based on what the perpetrator or other people said, is that source reliable?

Are you confusing a habit with a fact?

Does the belief seem true because you have said this to yourself so many times?

Are you using extreme ways of thinking by thinking in all or nothing terms or using exaggerated words or phrases?

Are you taking examples out of context by only considering one aspect of the situation at the expense of considering the entire incident?

Are you confusing a low probability with a high probability?

Are your judgments based on feelings rather than facts?

Are you drawing conclusions where evidence is lacking? Are you exaggerating (including catastrophizing) or minimizing the meaning of an event?

Are you overgeneralizing from a single event i.e. associating aspects of the assault or perpetrator to other areas of your life?

Are you mind reading other people's thoughts or intentions?

What is an alternative way of thinking about this situation?

How much do I believe my original thought now? a little medium a lot (or rate 0-100%)

What am I feeling now? angry sad anxious other How strong is the feeling? a little medium a lot (or rate 0-100%)

Consider the responses you gave to each question and determine the proper placement of the anxiety: Delegate, Eliminate, or Action plan.

Don't forget to breathe.

Day Eighteen:

Turning the Negative into a Positive

This can be a tough assignment however it is recommended to give it a try at the very least.

Consider something negative going on in your life, something that causes you worry or anxiety.

Make a list of 10 things about that negative life experience/event that are positive.

Note: try to avoid inverse positives that are only positive because they are related to the negative, ie "it could be worse, or at least it isn't as bad as 'this' experience." Try to focus on actual positives.

Once you have your list, look through each item and attempt to appreciate the positives of the negative experience/item, you are worried about.

Don't forget to breathe.

Day Nineteen:

A New Growth Experience

Much of anxiety has a lot to do with discomfort with the unknown or what is unfamiliar. It is why many people dread certain things they have never tried. This assignment isn't intended for you to go do something you are deathly afraid of, but to try something new or strange to you.

Take a few minutes and think about an action, activity, or experience you have not tried (or haven't tried in a very long time). Why have you avoided this action? What is stopping you now?

If possible, try to make a plan to do that activity, today if possible, or schedule it in your planner for a later day.

It could be a simple as having a conversation with someone, to as advanced as bungie jumping. The end is up to you, but try exploring your comfort zone and reach just beyond it.

Don't forget to breathe.

Day Twenty:

Today make a plan to do a journal entry.

It doesn't have to be written, but at least somehow recorded. Take a few minutes to write, type, text, film, or otherwise record a personal reflection of your worries, stresses, and anxiety.

Make a mental note of how you are feeling, and the way things have been going, for better or worse.

Reflect on the previous Journal entries and think about the progress toward your goals.

Don't forget to breathe.

Day Twenty-One:

Face your Fear I

Pick one Fear item from the list you previously made.

Today you will work on exposure to that fear.

Take at least one step into your discomfort toward that fear.

If you fear taking a trip, take a step by researching the cost and details of the trip, gather the information.

If you fear approaching a person, take the first step and plan out what you will say and when you might say it. Make a plan to talk to them.

If you fear getting a treatment or injection you need, look into it, practice with a safety pin lightly brushing against your skin. Remind yourself of how safe it is.

Use these examples to come up with a first step to take toward your own fears and take it.

Don't forget to breathe.

Day Twenty-Two:

What about my Money

Money and finances are easily the number one worry/anxiety for most adults. Money stress is often related to a focal point of having enough, at the right time, in the right circumstances. It is enough to make anyone anxious.

The entire thought process around it is one giant thinking error, however.

Today, take out a dollar bill, it can be any denomination, but a $1 is recommended to keep it simple.

Use a permanent marker and write on the bill "I appreciate my money."

As you do this, think about all the things that your money has provided for you, all the things you have and use. Stop for a moment throughout the day, look at that dollar bill and say "thank you" for all the things your money has given to you.

It is easy to be anxious about not having enough money, but appreciating the money you have, is the first step to freeing from the anxiety created by worry about it.

Leave that dollar somewhere that you can easily access it, and take it out and look at it whenever you feel you may be over stressing about money and remember all the things it has provided for you.

Don't forget to breathe

Day Twenty-Three:

Forgiveness

There is a saying that forgiveness isn't for the person being forgiven, it is for you. Forgiveness isn't always about releasing someone from their guilt or trespasses against you. In many way's forgiveness is the letting go of something that is being held on to; and the surrendering of that thought to the world outside oneself.

Today, think of something you are holding on to. Something from the past or even recent present that you have had trouble letting go of. It could be something someone did to you, or caused you to experience, or something you, yourself struggles with and are having trouble letting go of.

Today is that day.

Take some time to reflect on the thought. Picture it as a physical object or substance that can be taken and removed from your body. Visualize it, and let it go. Say the words "I forgive…." If it helps you or is relevant.

Today you will forgive and let go of a grudge or intruding thought you have been holding on to.

Don't forget to breathe

Day Twenty-Four:

Comfort over Comfort

Everyone has a comfort zone. It has been developed overtime through our experiences, victories, failures and even trauma.

Take some time today and think about your own comfort zone. Think of the areas where anxiety and your zone of comfort collide and where you feel your comfort zone holds you back from living the life you want.

It has been said that on the other side of your fear lies your happiness. That line will be a continuing trend moving forward from here.

Take one step today into the edges of your comfort zone.

This assignment gives you some flexibility and it can be more easy or more difficult depending on where you decide on.

Think of a course of action that will push you past your comfort zone in a small way that challenges the very way in which it has held you back from the life you want. Be confident in your decision and make an attempt at the very least.

Don't forget to breathe.

Day Twenty-Five:

Silence

It has been said that silence is golden. Sometimes however, silence can be more about what you hear when you are silent rather than the absents of sound.

Today's assignment involves conversation, so if you are spending the day alone, it is best to skip this day and do it on a day when you know you will interact with others.

In all conversation today, you will be silent. That is, you will listen to the other person speak and remain silent. You will not give encouraging nods, nor will you give active listening responses such as "uh-huh" or "yeah." You are to remain silent and when the person finishes speaking you will pause for 3 full seconds before responding.

This can be much harder than it sounds, especially if you are used to responding immediately. The idea here is that you want to calm your own anxiety of what you will say next and really focus on what the other person is saying without rehearsing your next words in your thoughts. Reflect on your experience and as always if you feel uncomfortable you can always use and easy out, such as "I'm just thinking" or some other response.

Don't forget to breathe.

Day Twenty-Six:

Safe Space

Sometimes when we are stressed or anxious a great strategy is to distract or mentally check out of the situation so that we can give our thoughts a break. Building a safe space is one such strategy to achieve this.

Sometime today find a quiet place where you can be alone for awhile and relax.

Sit comfortably and imagine a place where you do not feel anxious or stressed. The key features of your imagined place are that the scene is simple, repeating, and calming.

For example, some people picture a rock they have seen at the ocean, repeatedly hit by a wave. Try to imagine the smell, the sounds, and the sensation you feel when you are in this place.

Once you are satisfied with your created place (or memory of a real place), try to point out memorable details about it and key features so that you can easily take yourself back there when you need to.

The next time you feel stressed and can take a moment to yourself, try to imagine yourself in this place and relax.

Do your breathing assignment today while visualizing this place

Don't Forget to Breathe

Day Twenty-Seven:

Say No

Obligation is the cornerstone to stress and worry.

Today you are to practice saying no or more specifically, turning down, refusing, or delaying that which is assigned to you, obligated, or delegated.

In the tasks that you safely and reasonably are able to, just say no.

Today's tasks can be done in a variety of ways, but most will involved rescheduling, refusing, delegating, or otherwise rejecting an obligation that has been asked of you or placed upon you.

The obligations do not have to be specifics of just today, but anything you are actively engaged in or being asked of.

Don't forget to breathe.

Day Twenty-Eight:

Face Your Fear II

In the Face Your Fear I day, you took the first steps toward your fear, by researching, thinking about, or planning out a way to take on your fear.

In this next step, you will move a level past that. Today you will make a plan to take on the fear directly, but not actually attempt it.

You will look at days/time to face your fear.

You will practice taking the steps of the fear and working through each step in your mind.

You might talk to someone about it, or make phone calls or plans to initiate it.

Take the next step in exposing yourself to your fear. Don't forget to breathe.

Day Twenty-Nine

Today make a plan to do a journal entry.

It doesn't have to be written, but at least somehow recorded. Take a few minutes to write, type, text, film, or otherwise record a personal reflection of your worries, stresses, and anxiety.

Make a mental note of how you are feeling, and the way things have been going, for better or worse.

Reflect on the previous Journal entrys and think about the progress toward your goals.

Now that you are nearing the end of this thirty days, what did you learn? What challenges are you ready to push yourself to next?

Do not forget to breathe.

Day Thirty

Face your Fear III.

For thirty days you have challenged your worry, your fear, and explored aspects of yourself that have led to such stress.

Today you will face the fear directly.

Twice you have moved closer to exposing yourself to a fear, today you are ready to face and meet it head on.

Put yourself in a situation of discomfort and remember your skills and all the effort you have taken the last thirty days.

Remember, this should be a fear you can manage, but one that will challenge you.

Face it and let yourself move past its control over you.

Don't forget to breathe.

Going Forward

You've done it. You have finished the 30 days and challenged your worry and stress in meaningful and impactful ways.

Hopefully this book has taught you some useful tools and given you the chance to have some fun along the way as you challenge your own worries and stress.

Try to remember the key points from this book and utilize them in the future when you find they could be a benefit.

If you ever find that you lost your way or need a refreshed of the skills gone over in this book, simple check back and perhaps challenge yourself to another 30 days of positive change.

Remember, your anxiety was created in your own mind and you have the power over it.

Alexander R. Tipton holds a Masters in Counseling and a License in Professional Counseling and Therapy. Links and access to his other writings can be found at TiptonBooks.Webs.com or on Facebook, at Facebook.com/AlexanderRTpton

His Anxiety Management Course Can be found At Udemy.com under Managing Anxiety and Stress.

The book offers researched and time-tested strategies for reducing and controlling anxiety and stress. That said, it should not take the place of medical or other in-person mental health advice. This book exists solely for the purpose of self help and any advice or action taken as a result of this book is purely at the will/discretion of the reader. By taking part, the reader releases the author and distributor of all legal or ethical liability for any harm or damages that may result as a consequence of the information and homework assigned.

References

American Psychiatric Association (2000). *Diagnostic & statistical manual of mental disorders Behavior Modification, 31*(5), 595-615.

Elkins, S. R., & Moore, T. M. (2011). A time-series study of the treatment of panic disorder. *Clinical Case Studies, 10*(1), 3-22.

Fernandez, I. & Faretta, E. (2007). Eye movement desensitization and reprocessing in the treatment of panic disorder with agoraphobia. *Clinical Case Studies, 6*(1), 44-63.

Goodwin, E. A. & Montgomery, D. D. (2006). A cognitive-behavioral, biofeedback-assisted relaxation treatment for panic disorder with agoraphobia. *Clinical Case Studies, 5*(2), 112-125.

Haun, J. & Truax, M. (2007). Cognitive behavior therapy for atypical generalized anxiety disorder (GAD): When functional assessment reveals social fears function, such as worry, in GAD. *Clinical Case Studies. 6(3)*, 195-217.

Labreque, J., Marchand, A., Dugas, M.J., & Letarte, A. (2007). Efficacy of cognitive-behavioral therapy for co-morbid panic disorder with agoraphobia and generalized anxiety disorder. *Behavior Modification, 31*(5). 616-637.

Meuret, A. E., Wilhelm, F. H., Ritz, T., & Roth W. T. (2003). Breathing training for treating panic disorder: useful intervention of impediment? *Behavior Modification, 27*(5), 731-754.

Miyatani, Y. (2005). On understanding the being of panic disorder patients. *Journal of Humanistic Psychology, 45*(1), 54-61.

Peres, M., Lucchetti, G., Mercante, J., & Young, W. B. (2011). New daily persistent headache and panic disorder. *Cephalalgia, 31(*2), 250-253.

Roberge, P., Marchand, A. Reinharz, D., & Sacard, P. (2008). Cognitive-behavioral treatment for panic disorder with agoraphobia: a randomized, controlled trial and cost-effectiveness analysis. *Behavioral Modification, 32*(3), 333-351.

, *4th ed, TR*, Washington DC: Author.

Deacon, B. (2007). Two-day, intensive cognitive-behavioral therapy for panic disorder: a case study.

www.ingramcontent.com/pod-product-compliance
Lightning Source LLC
Chambersburg PA
CBHW061513250726
48657CB00005B/1831